Dear Life

Archana Pimpalnerkar
Kulkarni

BookLeaf
Publishing

India | USA | UK

Presentation by *BookLeaf Publishing*

Web: www.bookleafpub.com

E-mail: info@bookleafpub.com

Illustrations: Archana Pimpalnerkar Kulkarni

Cover page photograph: Archana Pimpalnerkar Kulkarni

ISBN: 9789360949181

First edition 2024

DEDICATION

To my parents,

You are my inspiration and strength every
single day.

I would like to thank my mother for showing
me the beauty of poetry and giving me strength
and my father for showing me what courage
and enthusiasm is and being my guiding light.

ACKNOWLEDGEMENT

This book would not have been possible without my family and the few dear friends who knew I wrote. My husband, Rupen and sons, Tanay and Arnav have encouraged me to follow my dreams and kept me motivated. I am ever so grateful for your love, support and for believing in me.

PREFACE

Only when one can read the words in a poem for what they express, the poem comes alive and touches you from within.

CONTENTS

Something About The Train

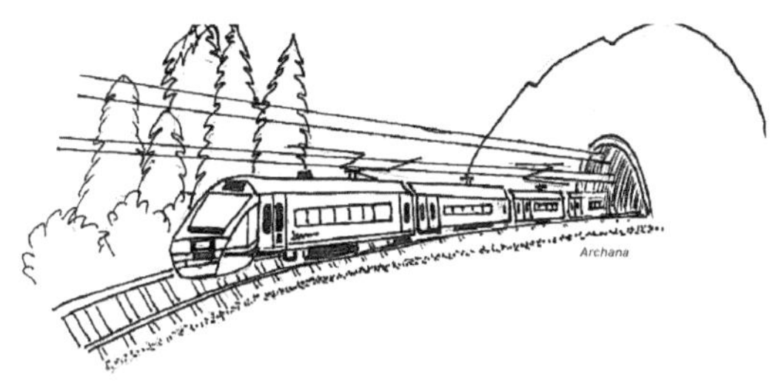

Something about the train
makes me think

The fields whizz by
but the mind stands still

I'm moving ahead
as the thoughts seep in

Somewhere in the movement
there is a stillness
where it all blends in

Something about the train
makes me think

There's an eagerness to get ahead
while past memories flood in

Quick glimpses of the world
fade past in a hurry

Somewhere between the rails
between the future and the past
the present nicely settles in

Something about the train
makes me think.

Wonder Why

Often wonder why
we do the things we do
Is there a reason
a hidden meaning
or just things we must do?

Often wonder why
we think the way we do
Caring and sharing
just being there for dear ones as we do

Often wonder why
we sometimes care so much
That it burns us inside
as the pain simmers up

Often wonder why
it's us that have this pain
Perhaps 'cos we are meant to
or we are blessed with strength to take the strain

Often wonder why
life is so beautiful
Nothing to regret, fear or hide
simple sweet and peaceful

Often wonder if things had been different
would they have been as pretty
Half as much as joyous
Shared with the same people

Yes, I wonder why
the world is so mysteriously magical
As we bow our heads in humility,
fill our hearts with pride
and accept life's challenges placed by our side.

Memories Fade

Another day goes by
the road seems so far
Will it lead you far away
and the memories start to fade?

Another day goes by
nothing seems the same
Will the face be a blur
Will the heart still stir?

Another day goes by
the memory brings a smile
the feeling is still alive
Somewhere deep inside
you will always stay alive.

Rest a While

Rest your heavy head a while
your tired thoughts spill over
Melt the troubles on your pillow
and let sleep take over

Rest your tired legs a while
let the aches melt away
The road has just begun my friend
a long journey awaits

Rest your aching hands for now
rub out harsh words written
Breathe in some fresh energy
and kind letters re-written

Rest a little while my friend
dream a little dream
With the morning sunshine
may the day follow that dream.

You Will Never Know

A little twinkle
a little smile
You never know
it can last a mile

A little touch
a gentle kiss
You'll never know
if you give it a miss

Life's far too short
to wonder why
We'll never know
if we don't try.

Dreams

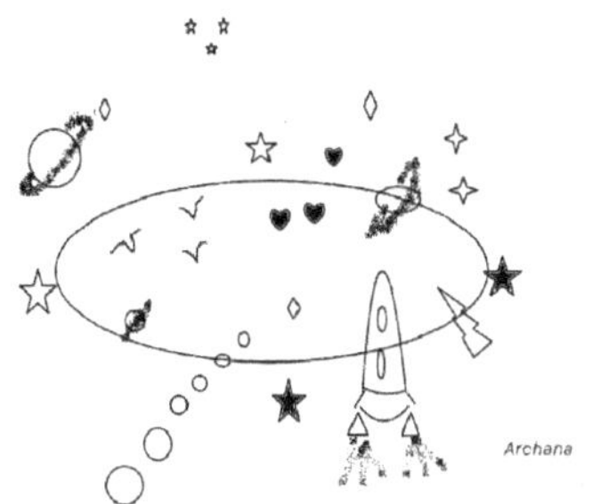

It's a funny thing about dreams
they are ever so real
Take you places you want to be
see faces ever so clear

It's a funny thing about dreams
you can have anything
Feel the fire and the rain,
even the hate and the pain

It's a funny thing about dreams
find the places of peace
Be the person you want to be
perhaps even never leave

It's a funny thing about dreams
you can say the sorry you never did
Feel happiness instead of fear
thank the friends that were dear

Yes, it's a funny thing about dreams.

To a Poet Born

The poet weaves with her words
all the beauty that she sees
Turns the simplest things
into incredible dreams

The poet weaves with her smile
a million happy moments
Brightens up the world
with her little naughty giggles

The poet weaves with her voice
so sweet and kind and sure
A thousand hearts strung
with love so pure

The poet weaves with her strength
through life's ups and downs
Standing rock steady
to face challenges so profound

The poet weaves for her friends
a net of joy and happiness
Keeping hearts alive
with wisdom and wittiness

The poet weaves her words
spontaneous and so pure
Not realising how her magic
reaches each and every ear.

The Silence

I can hear so much in your silence
I long to hear more again

What you aren't telling me is the loneliness
the fear and dread of your pain

The weakness that encompasses your body
the clouded sigh of your brain

Your fight to feel better and stronger
despite the cancer and heart
playing their games

Your eyes widen with hope
searching for clarity and answers
Your arms still reach out to comfort
and offer words to ease others' pain

I can hear so much in your silence
and can see the man young again

A smile on your lips
beaming through your eyes
cheeks pink with joy

'Enjoy!' you say, 'every moment,'
'It's a new wonderful day!'

The simplest of things make you giggle
nature's wonder got you amazed

Each person you met never forgot you
because you treated each one like the best again

Your magic handshake is a child's delight
a bond that will always remain

I can hear so much in your silence
how life taught you to be brave

The struggles of childhood you challenged
with quiet dignity and pride

Working through tender ages
bringing in food with humble pride

The eldest of four you battled on
with kindness and grace in your heart

Where most would be hardened by fate
you silently worked on unphased

I can hear so much in your silence
I long to see more again

The man with eternal enthusiasm
sharing joy where ever he goes
The man with detailed precision
and respect for efforts
that life makes one unfold

A man with an amazing vision
ahead of his time
which many could not behold

A man with so much forgiveness
so friendly, loving and kind

I can hear so much in your silence Dad
I want to hold you and hear it all again.

If Time Stood Still

If time stood still
would bees still sting
would wounds still hurt
would memories burn?

If life stood still
would people alter
would dreams shatter
would moments still matter?

If time stood still
would rivers run
would wind blow
would laughter echo?

If life stood still
would opportunities arise
would miracles arrive
would love survive?

Paragliding

Higher and higher we lift to the skies
as the wings catch the wind
Once past the sudden rise
everything almost stands still

There is calm in air
not a single care
leaving the worries behind

Just the valleys below
in their majestic glow
Cradling the river
as it bends and flows

We all have our different stories
like the varied colours of our wings
We all take different journeys
and different dreams within

Sometimes higher we fly, sometimes lower
gently swerve to the left or the right
Harnessing the wind is not an option
remember to surrender and trust in the flight.

Deepest of Fears

Deepest of fears, why do you toss and turn?
You burn like the ember
that scorches and burns.

Deepest of fears, why do you mock me so?
You take me through terrors
I have never been before

You race wild through the years
woven tender and strong
by moments so precious
only the fragrance lingers on

Deepest of fears, why do you take me apart?
You show me the pain
while tearing a piece of my heart

You take me through horrors so very alone
Sans family, sans loving home
Deepest of fears, I toss you aside
but I hear you snigger at life's inevitable lies.

The Sparrow

Ah, there's a little puddle
that is perfect just for me

To wash my little feathers
and wet my tired feet

I'm sure I'll find a grain or two
perhaps a juicy bug

A little something is all I need
and perhaps a little hug

I like being a little happy
 and doing a merry hop

The sun is out and shining
I'm off to do a job

I'll fly over the hilltops
Take a stop on a tree or two

Chat with other birdlings
share a seed with them too

I'll try my quickest flapping
feel the breeze upon my chest

Admire the mighty waterfall
and all the world at its best

Oh, what a lovely job I have
flying here and there

Experiencing life's great wonders
without any other care

Ah, here's a bigger puddle
that's perfect just for me

I'll jump in a little deeper
Knowing life is testing me.

Preoccupied

The mind's a cloud of clutter
nothing seems so clear

Places that I used to frequent
things that I felt dear

What used to be so easy
now's a ton more difficult to steer

I am told, I am full of it
preoccupied and queer

Each one sees it different
sees me wasting all my time

Ailing parents aren't an easy sight
each demand seems a fright

My body is so tired
the mind seems quite tight

I should really feel happy
but it's like I've run a mile

I am told I am full of it
of quite a sorry mind

The time will pass when all is done
and there's nothing left to do

I will hang my head in surrender then
and accept it as cue

I will find myself again I guess
empty head and heart

As life goes on once more
I shall try again to play my part.

Tiger cubs

The jungle's where the tiger cubs
play and learn to stalk their game

Watching every movement
each pause and pounce again

The hard day's training now is done
the heat tires them out

A quick nap in the shade is all it takes
as they bounce up and run about

Young at heart
not a fear in sight
every hunt for them is a game

What fun for the brothers
to chase each other,
wrestle hard and tug at the steak

The jungle's where the tiger cubs
dare to test their play

Chase the deer, wild boar and buffalo
feel grand as they shadow their prey

They will learn from the sound
of the gunshot afar
Their safety lies deep in the leaves

To tune their ears and senses sharp
and wait in the thicket deep

The jungle's where the tiger cubs
live a life so free

And it's the jungle where it all begins and ends
this amazing world of the beasts.

Evening Stars

I blow the stars a little kiss
and wish and hope they don't miss

I wink an eye at the rising sun
 and ask the dew drop on my nose not to run

I listen hard at the slightest breeze
and make up sentences that you might speak

I ask the bee of the things he's seen
 and the bird of faraway places he's been

I look at the world, a million times over
and search every nook
every cranny and clover

And there on an island of my imagination
 amidst an oasis of memories and dreams

I see my loved one hale and hearty
blowing a kiss to the stars just for me.

Today

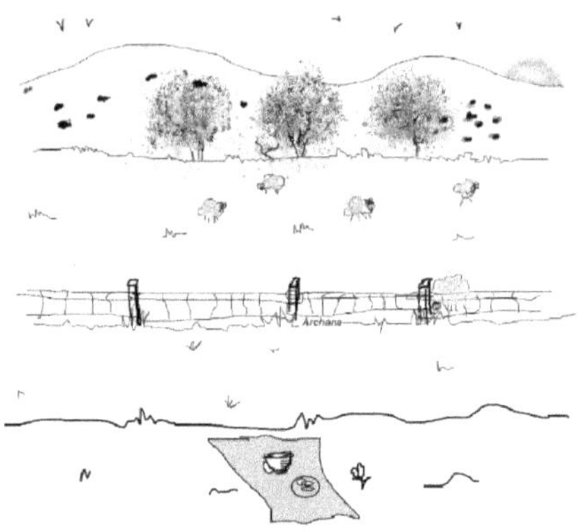

Today I can see the sun in the sky
and feel the crisp fresh air

Every breath fills my chest
and blows away all care

The cup of tea I take for granted
the biscuit that melts in my mouth

The warm hugs of good morning
the words of wisdom read aloud

Today I can walk in the garden
with some aches still about

I see bulls in the pasture
and sheep grazing by the fence

I notice pears and apples
and smell blossom on the trees

Swallows fly into tiny corners
while sparrows make their nests

Today I have a simple life
yet the very best

'Today' is really all I have
so, let's forget the rest.

Mother Dear

I see your strength
as you battle along
with a walking frame in hand

Going about the daily chores
and lending a helping hand

The times have changed
the tables turned
now it's all up to you

Where once you were looked after
with so much care
now it's your turn too

Your speed is slow
your temper blows
the fiery speech cuts deep

It's a difficult time
a test of time
You can't always hide it
with your busy deeds

May be pause a while
let things go
cherish the moments you have

You won't have what you got
for very long
don't let unsaid things be lost

I see your strength
as you keep sharp
though fear is clouding your brain

Forgive all the past misgivings
and live each day
as a gift despite the pain

Keep your strength dear
it's a fact of life
cherish what is here today
Who knows what tomorrow brings
some sunshine or inevitable rain.

Just a Poem

There is nothing fancy here to write
no flamboyant words

Just a feeling that finds its way out
in very simple terms

Doesn't matter where I am
by the hills or sea

Perhaps waiting in line
when I have somewhere else to be

The words get stuck in my head
like bottled up feelings

Sometimes never even know
that's how I'm really feeling.

There's nothing fancy here to write
no dramatic lines

Just the ones that come from the heart
some happy, funny or sublime

Sometimes the rhythm isn't there
a cluttered muddled read

But then I often find
true words lie deep within.

Living Obituary

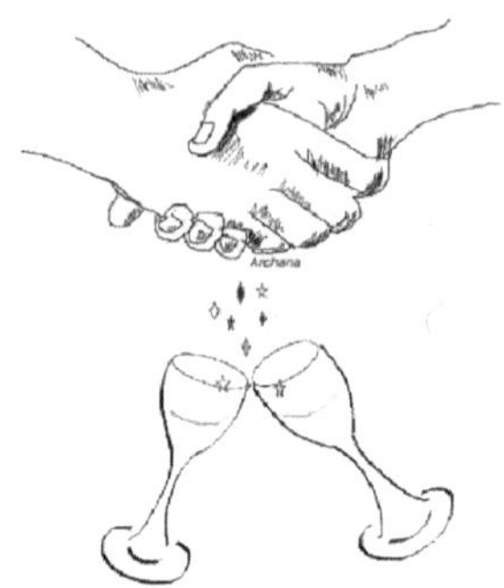

Oh, dear friend would you like to hear
what I have to say?
Why wait for the coldness of the grave!

A jolly friend
time well spent
You always are so funny

Someone I can count on
someone rock steady

A heart of gold
so, you've been told
I would add on some more topping

Larger than life
Oh! what a life
and such an amazing buddy

So, before you depart
let's shake hands and
share a few more jokes

Remember old times
and raise your glass for a jolly toast
To my old friend, my good friend
Cheers!! Here's one for the road!

Tough in Vain

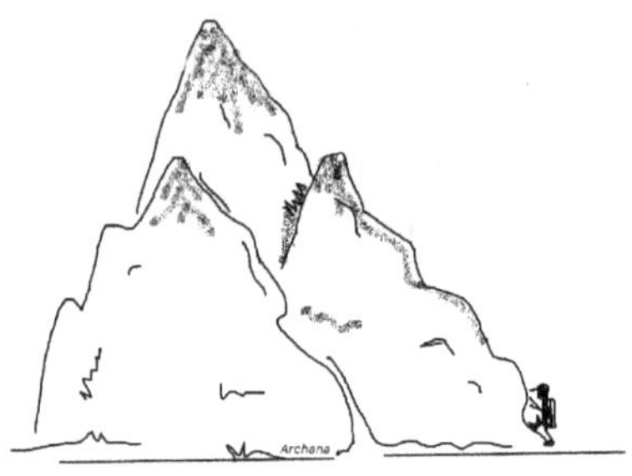

I see it in your eyes
as you mock and scorn
you see no other as 'Highly born'!
As the mountain in the heavenly mist
every living creature to
you seems diseased!

Human touch, purest of thoughts
kind respect and humble homes
To the untouchable peak
seem so trivial and meek

Behold! Oh, proud mountain
unbending and cold
'tis lonely and deathly
your domineering abode

How much of the natural spring
can you withhold
as it giggles and trickles away

Thrust into the height of your own free will
aiming for the gifts of heaven
which are actually deep within

Hurling all away as you search for the warmth
Oh! Foolish stone, why can't you see
Heaven is here in every heart to seek

Scratch deep is your glory
though true, you have achieved
Staunch through disaster
your footing is only so deep

But mightiest of mightiest
you lose more than you keep
Love and laughter are heaven's gift
to the tiniest of beasts.

Being Alive

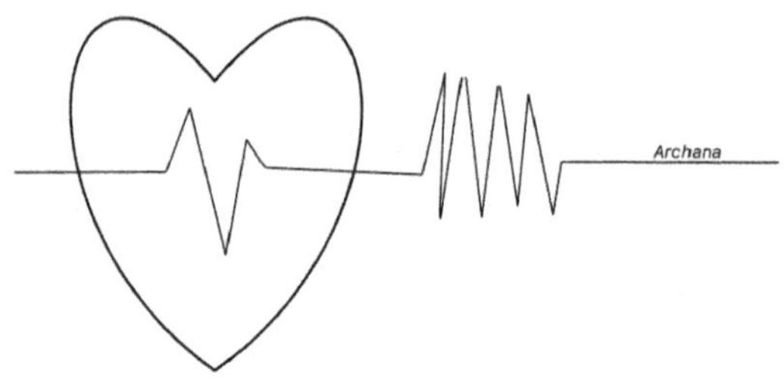

Just one look before I sleep

Before I miss a heart beat

Before I realise you are not there

Before I wake from the dream that I do not dare

Be Kind

When it is one of those days
When the mind is clouded or in pain
When you don't really know what to say
And clutter takes over the brain
Remember then that less is more
Try to keep an open door
And if harshness ever comes to mind
'When in doubt, be kind.'

Dear Life

Oh, dear child you show me
what life is all about
Your big wide eyes amazed and bright
with wonder and delight

Your giggles and your laughter
run along the rivers to the sea
While the wind blows your paper boat
far beyond what you can see

Each tiny step is walking truly far ahead
Those tiny fingers stronger
now caress my aching head
The little cuddle grew fast into a warm embrace
I was watching your little games
now I'm admiring your grace

Oh, dear child you know how to live this life
Your brave heart leads you on
to dreams and ambitions high
Pause for a moment and remember then
You have always been
the dearest part of my life.